IMAGES
of America

KEARNY'S
IMMIGRANT HERITAGE

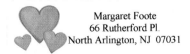

Margaret Foote
66 Rutherford Pl.
North Arlington, NJ 07031

TWO PIPERS. Pipers have lent Kearny a distinctive ethnic flavor for more than a century. (Courtesy Jock Nisbet.)

IMAGES
of America

KEARNY'S
IMMIGRANT HERITAGE

Barbara Krasner

To Margaret,
Always take pride in your heritage
and in Kearny's heritage.
Best,
Barbara
3/9/04

ARCADIA

Published by Arcadia Publishing,
an imprint of Tempus Publishing Inc.
Portsmouth NH, Charleston SC, Chicago,
San Francisco

Printed in Great Britain

Library of Congress Catalog Card Number: 2003111117

For all general information, contact Arcadia Publishing:
Telephone 843-853-2070
Fax 843-853-0044
E-mail sales@arcadiapublishing.com
For customer service and orders:
Toll-free 1-888-313-2665

Visit us on the Internet at www.arcadiapublishing.com

A GAME OF MULTICULTURAL CHESS. Today, kids from all over the world attend Kearny High School. Here, five students play chess during lunch period, each representing a different country of birth: America, Poland, Guyana, Brazil, and Portugal. (Courtesy Patti Sapone/the Star-Ledger.)

4

CONTENTS

ACKNOWLEDGMENTS

This book would not be possible without the help and generosity of a variety of individuals and organizations. Unlike the first volume on Kearny, which drew primarily from the collections of the Kearny Museum and Kearny Free Public Library, *Kearny's Immigrant Heritage* relied on cultural associations and members of specific ethnic groups. It is their story I tell. If a particular ethnic group is not represented here, it is only due to a lack of photographs and does not convey in any way a lack of contribution to the community.

I owe the concept of this book to Mayor Alberto Santos, who perhaps unknowingly suggested it with his letter to me about the first book. This project could not have been successfully completed without his personal assistance and the help of Ron Novis and others in his office and town administration. I continue to owe a debt of gratitude to Charlie Waller and George Rogers, who made the holdings of the Kearny Museum available to this project. George also provided photographs and genealogies of his family. I must also thank Elena Nakrosis, Our Lady of Sorrows Church and the Schuyler Savings Bank; Tony Cardoso and the Portuguese Cultural Association; Jock and Joan Nisbet of Argyle Fish & Chips; Susan Leahy Jutkiewicz and the Leahy family of the Thistle; Paddy Burke; the Irish American Club; Bill Hutcheson and the Copestone Masonic Temple; Ed and Cathy Burns and the First Evangelical Lutheran Church; Mayra Santos; Rita Norberg; John O'Hara and Arlene Sheldrick of the Kearny School District; Alexa Arce; Gordon and Joan Sprengel Kimball; and the many Kearny High School alumni who contributed their family histories and photographs, including Harold and Randy Bjorken, Marianne Jacullo Brosnan, Chris Coccia, Fred Gillespie, Arthur Hawkinson, James Kazalis, Bob Kirk, Christina Mihalis Kozinski, Ed Leonard, Larry Levy, Kenneth Lundstrom, Tomika Masui, Minna Bogner Nelson, Norman Prestup, Craig and Roseanne Carchidi Stewart, the Leahy family (Michael, Carole, and Bill), Maurice Viscuso, Walt Whimpenny, and Tada and Seiko Yamaguchi. Thanks for your response to my e-mail and telephone requests.

I would also like to acknowledge Joe Settani, archivist at the Jewish Historical Society of MetroWest, the staff of the New Jersey Information Center at the Newark Public Library, Carla Giannoble at the *Star-Ledger* photograph library, and Bill Bayer of the *Kearny, Harrison, and East Newark Journal*.

Acknowledgments of photograph sources are noted in each caption.

Finally, I'd like to express my appreciation to Anne de Ocejo for pushing me to do this book, to Scott Jacobs for his technical support, and to my family and friends for their continued encouragement and support.

INTRODUCTION

Mention the town of Kearny and someone will respond with soccer, Argyle Fish & Chips, or a bagpipe band. But the town also has a rich mixture of cultures that includes central, eastern, and southern Europe; Latin America; and Asia. Situated at the crossroads of larger cities Jersey City and Newark and at the crossroads of major transportation modes, Kearny continues to serve as a crossroads of cultures.

Since its Lenni Lenape beginning as Mighgecticok, Kearny has welcomed waves of newcomers to America. The land was first sold by Chief Tantaqua to Capt. William Sandford of Barbados in 1668.

Kearny attracted Scots in 1875, when Clark Thread of Paisley, Scotland, opened two mills in town and encouraged thousands of workers to immigrate. In 1883, the Marshall Flax Spinning Company of England erected a large plant in Kearny and called for flax spinners from other parts of the British Isles, most notably Ireland. Other Scottish businesses opened American branches in Kearny, particularly Nairn Linoleum Company in 1888 and Barbour Flax. Eventually, a community formed around commerce, customs, and fellowship. By the 1920s, streetcar conductors announced "Paisley Cross" when they reached the intersection of Kearny and Bergen Avenues. The term derived from the Glasgow suburb of Paisley, the origin of many of Kearny's Scottish immigrants. Parishioners flocked to Knox Presbyterian, St. Cecilia's, and St. Stephen's Churches and lived predominantly in the town's first and second wards.

Other significant immigrant communities began to emerge. The Union organized for people wanting to conduct church services in Swedish in 1883. A Methodist church was established in December 1896. Baptist members of the Union started their own church in August 1889, and the Church of Gustavas Vasa, which became the Swedish Evangelical Lutheran Church, formed in 1890.

The Lithuanian community in the Kearny area dates back to 1895 and has roots predominantly from the Suvalkijos and Dzukijos provinces. Kearny attracted Lithuanians because of its ample building space, rural settings, and proximity to the many industries of Harrison and Newark. The community established Our Lady of Sorrows Church, the parish school, the Schuyler Savings Bank, and the Lithuanian Catholic Community Center.

Also from Lithuania was Kearny's first Jew, Jack Cashel, in 1879. He changed his name to Goldstein and opened a dry-goods store at the lower end of Kearny Avenue. His brother Israel followed and he opened another dry-goods store at 146 Midland. Other immigrant Jewish families came to Kearny after first settling in Newark or Jersey City.

A large number of Italians from Calabria and Naples found Kearny to be a good place to live. Japanese families made their homes in Kearny in the early 1900s.

Although many of Kearny's cultural heritages are mere whispers today, the immigrant and assimilation process remains similar. Just as children in the 1960s and earlier may have felt coerced by their parents to attend Scottish dancing school, today's children may feel the same as they attend Portuguese dancing school. Today, the town raises the Italian flag in October in honor of Christopher Columbus, the Lithuanian flag in February to commemorate independence, the Irish flag to celebrate St. Patrick's Day, and the Portuguese flag in June to initiate Portugal Day.

Ever at the crossroads of culture, Kearny represents the American melting pot. Its residents recently reported an ancestry of 13 percent Irish, 12 percent Italian, 12 percent Portuguese, 8 percent Polish, 6 percent German, and 3 percent Scottish. Kearny's varied heritage produced three World Cup soccer players for the 1990 games alone: Tony Meola of Italian heritage, Tab Ramos of Uruguayan heritage, and John Harkes of Scottish heritage.

Kearny's Immigrant Heritage presents a long-awaited history never widely shared beyond specific cultural boundaries. Drawing on numerous interviews with associations and families representing diverse ethnic groups, this history also sheds light on the impact that the town's multiculturalism has made on its community.

One

THE BRITISH ISLES

SOCCERTOWN, USA. For more than 100 years, soccer has found a home in Kearny's immigrant culture. Here, members of the Scots-American team of 1946 pose on Kearny Avenue. They are, from left to right, as follows: (kneeling) Alex Campbell and Russ Brown; (standing) Steve Hudi, Stewart Aitken, Alex Rae, and George Rogers. (Courtesy Kearny Museum.)

WILLIAM GREEN. Born in Bath, Somerset, England, in 1845, William Green was a prominent businessman and public official in Kearny. A successful realtor, he served as a member of the town committee of Kearny, the street and water commissioner, a member and later director of the Hudson County Board of Chosen Freeholders, a member of Copestone Lodge of Free and Accepted Masons of West Hudson, and a member of the Fort Laurel Lodge of Foresters of Americas of Arlington.

GEORGE CUNLIFFE. George Cunliffe was born in Lancashire, England, in 1847. He came to the United States in 1880 to work in the Clark Thread mills. He is perhaps best known for developing botanic beer, for which he built a trade and factory in Kearny.

CLARK'S MILE END. John Clark Jr. & Company of Glasgow, Scotland, formed an American company, the Clark Mile End Spool Cotton Company in 1878, augmenting the East Newark mills of the Clark Thread Company (of Paisley, Scotland). The spinning and twisting of thread took place in these buildings. Thousands of immigrants came to the area to work in these mills and other parts of the Clark Thread Company. (Courtesy Norman Prestup.)

MEN AT WORK. Clark Thread of Scotland brought an estimated 2,000 Scots to the area to work in its Newark, Kearny, and Harrison facilities. Many came from Paisley on Scotland's west coast. In 1900, most of Kearny's adults worked at Clark Thread. The Kearny plant employed 860 people by 1900 and 1,200 by 1918. George Rogers Sr. stands on the extreme right. (Courtesy George Rogers.)

AN OPPORTUNITY FOR WORK. John Sloan, born in 1879, came from Shannon, Ireland, to work in the Clark Thread mills. He and his wife, Mary, lived at 81 Woodland Avenue. (Courtesy Maurice Viscuso.)

NAIRN CONGOLEUM. In 1887, Sir Michael Nairn of Scotland established the Nairn Linoleum Company in Kearny and brought over many artisans to work there. The company was known for many years as Nairn Congoleum and then as Congoleum, although it was known as "the Nairn" to many Kearnians. The last vestiges of the factory buildings were demolished in 1976.

THE AMERICAN DREAM. Wilfred Gillespie Sr. left Rothesay, Scotland, in June 1947, leaving his wife, Jean MacMillan Gillespie, and their three sons (two of whom, William and Fred, are shown here) to take a job in Kearny with Nairn. After only three months, Wilfred sent for his family, wiring them to sell everything to pay for the flight over. Like many immigrants, they arrived with only the shirts on their backs. (Courtesy Fred Gillespie.)

THE MARSHALL FLAX MILLS. In 1883, the Marshall Flax Spinning Company of England erected a large plant in Kearny and called for flax spinners from other parts of the British Isles to work there. (Courtesy Norman Prestup.)

PAISLEY ABBEY. This embroidered depiction of the beloved Paisley Abbey pays tribute to the many Scots who left the thread-making culture of Paisley to begin anew in Kearny. (Courtesy Jock Nisbet.)

PAISLEY CROSS, 1968. The corner of Kearny and Bergen Avenues was known as Paisley Cross because men from Paisley in Scotland gathered there each afternoon to share stories. Here, three immigrants exchange bits of news from their home across the ocean. (Courtesy Newark Public Library.)

A BIT OF NEWS FROM HOME, 1968. Transplanted Scots Claude Nielsen (seated) of Hamilton and George Blackie of Paisley, who settled in Kearny in 1924, read a Glasgow newspaper in Town Hall Park. (Courtesy Newark Public Library.)

AT THE SCOTTISH BAKERY, 1968. Pamela Vallance of Ayr County, Scotland, with her daughter Susan in tow scans the goodies at Balmoral Bakery. The bakery was owned by David Donohoe of Saltcoast and his wife, Jeanie, of Renfrew. (Courtesy Newark Public Library.)

A LITTLE PIECE OF HOME, 1968. Catherine McGonnigle, a native of Renfrew who came to America in the 1920s, scans imported foods, saying, "After all these years, my husband and I still like all this food most of the time. It seems to—well—have a better flavor." (Courtesy Newark Public Library.)

A Scottish Meat Market, 1968. Cameron's Meat Shop on Kearny Avenue was a frequent stop for women such as Mrs. William Ritchie Gross, who stocks up on Scottish goodies— tripe, meat pies, and steak sausage—to take home to her family. The store was managed by Claude Nielsen. (Courtesy Newark Public Library.)

The Copestone Masonic Temple. Over the years, the Masonic lodge on Kearny Avenue south of Bergen Avenue has had a high membership of Scots. In fact, some named it "the Scots Lodge." (Courtesy Norman Prestup.)

On Parade. Members of the Copestone Masonic Temple proudly march in one of the town's many parades. (Courtesy George Rogers.)

The Knights Templar. An integral part of the Masonic fraternity, the Knights Templar, seen parading along Kearny Avenue, belonged to an organization that was based on an 11th-century group. (Courtesy Kearny Museum.)

SCOTTISH HERITAGE AFLOAT. The Monarch Savings Bank took advantage of Kearny's Scottish heritage on its float in Kearny's centennial celebration in 1967. (Courtesy Kearny Museum.)

THE SCOTS-AMERICAN CLUB FLOAT. The Scots-American Club and youngsters of Scottish heritage pay homage to the town in Kearny's centennial celebration. (Courtesy Kearny Museum.)

THE REGULARS. The Scots-American Club, founded in 1931 at 40 Patterson Street, was and still is a frequent stomping ground for its regulars. Tommy Cameron, like many of the regulars, takes his regular seat. (Courtesy Susan Leahy Jutkiewicz.)

INSIDE THE SCOTS-AMERICAN CLUB. Seen here are, from front to back, Tommy McAllister, former president of the Irish-American Club; Owen Higney, who found local sponsor homes for the Glasgow Celtic Boys; Richie McDermott; and Frank McAllister. (Courtesy Susan Leahy Jutkiewicz.)

THE THISTLE. Annie McCurley bought the Thistle from Charlie and Peg Levins in the late 1960s. Julie and Jerry Leahy took it over in 1977. Today, their son Bill Leahy, a chef, continues to serve up traditional fish and chips and more to the restaurant's patrons. (Courtesy Susan Leahy Jutkiewicz.)

THE GLASGOW CELTICS. The Thistle sponsored the Glasgow Celtic Boys to play here, much to the delight of the local female teenagers. Most of the boys went on to play professionally in Scotland. (Courtesy Susan Leahy Jutkiewicz.)

IN FRIENDSHIP. Inside the Thistle, owner Jerry Leahy extends a gesture of goodwill to the Glasgow Celtic Boys. (Courtesy Susan Leahy Jutkiewicz.)

ADDRESSING THE HAGGIS. Each year at Argyle Fish & Chips, people flock to participate in the annual Addressing the Haggis ceremony, part of the birthday celebration of Scottish poet Robert Burns. (Courtesy Jock Nisbet.)

THE KEARNY CALEDONIAN PIPE BAND. Sporting the MacBeth tartan in this official photograph, the band began as the Fairleigh Dickinson University Pipe Band. Jock Nisbet, who came to Kearny from Scotland in the 1950s and is currently co-owner of Argyle Fish & Chips, stands in the front row on the far right. (Courtesy Jock Nisbet.)

MAYOR ROWLANDS AND THE KEARNY CALEDONIAN PIPE BAND. Seen here are, from left to right, the following: (front row) Hank Girdwood, Bill Mogensen, Ernie Alexander, John ?, Mayor Dave Rowlands, Bob Pollock, George Adams, and Sandy Graham; (back row) Al Kennedy, Jim McQuilkin, Allan McQuilkin, Tom Brancella, Joe McConville, Roy Cook, Jean-Claud Aloux, Jim Edmonds, Jock Nisbet, and Bobby Brown. (Courtesy Jock Nisbet.)

NO SCOTTISH TABLE? Kearny High School alum and math teacher Walt Whimpenny sports the hunting tartan of the Fraser clan at the 2003 Kearny High School International Festival, a tradition he began when the festival needed someone at the Scottish table. Whimpenny's grandfather, also Walter Whimpenny, arrived in America from Oldham, England, in 1904. He worked at "the Nairn." (Courtesy Kearny School District.)

TARTANS, ARGYLES, AND PIPES. What Kearny parade would be complete without the traditional tartan kilts and bagpipe band? (Courtesy Kearny Museum.)

THE HIGHLAND FLING. Marie Johanhans performs in a Highland dance competition. (Courtesy Jock Nisbet.)

THE BAGPIPE BAND, 1967. Jay McGonigal salutes as he and his band head north toward Midland Avenue. (Courtesy Kearny Museum.)

THE ST. COLUMCILLE UNITED GAELIC PIPE BAND, 1976. Still functioning today, this band provides consistent entertainment in Kearny's parades. (Courtesy Kearny Museum.)

KILTS FOR RENT. Renting a tuxedo for a wedding is not for everyone. The Pipers Cove routinely rents kilts for such important occasions. (Courtesy Jock Nisbet.)

BAGPIPES FOR HIRE. As long as you are renting a kilt, why not hire a piper? Jock Nisbet, featured here, offers bagpipes, pipe bands, and dancers for all occasions, including weddings, funerals, and parties. (Courtesy Jock Nisbet.)

A Tartan for Everyone. If you need a tartan, just visit the Pipers Cove, adjacent to Argyle Fish & Chips on Kearny Avenue. Although there are more than 1,100 named tartans representing distinctive Scottish families and districts, only about 200 to 300 are commonly sold today. (Courtesy Jock Nisbet.)

WHAT IS A PHOTOGRAPH WITHOUT A PIPER? Seen here are, from left to right, unidentified, Fran Raftery, Jerry Leahy, unidentified, Sonny McKeown, and Paddy Brannigan. (Courtesy Susan Leahy Jutkiewicz.)

THE BELFAST SOCIAL CLUB. In top hats and tails, this group is set to march in the 1938 St. Patrick's Day parade. Although their banner reads "Harrison," many of the club's members were Kearnians, including George Patrick Leonard, the fourth man from the right, who came from Belfast in northern Ireland in the 1920s. His son, Edmund, the boy in front on the right, joins his cousin, Thomas McCloskey, who stands in front of his father, Daniel. (Courtesy Ed Leonard.)

THE IRISH AMERICAN CLUB. The Irish American Club formed in 1933 to create a place where Kearny's Irish immigrants could meet and relax. It also provided a center for social activities

ANNUAL PICNIC
IRISH-AMERICAN CLUB
ISLAND BEACH   AUG. 13, 1961

such as this outing for its members to Island Beach in 1961. (Courtesy Irish American Club.)

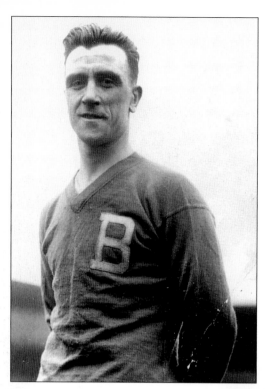

ARCHIBALD MACPHERSON "ARCHIE" STARK. A native of Glasgow, Scotland, Stark arrived in America in 1912 at the age of 14. He lived on Highland Avenue and played for Kearny's Scots-American and Irish-American soccer teams as well as on the United States team in 1925. The "B" on his uniform stands for Bethlehem Steel, a team he also played on. He was inducted into the National Soccer Hall of Fame in 1950 and died in Kearny in 1985. (Courtesy Kearny Museum.)

DAVID "DAVEY" BROWN. Davey Brown was born to Scottish immigrant parents and lived on Duke Street. He played soccer in international games in 1925 and 1926. He is shown here in his uniform for a game against Canada in 1926. He entered the National Soccer Hall of Fame in 1951 and died in Kearny in 1970. (Courtesy Kearny Museum.)

A Celebration of Soccer. Young soccer champions go along for the ride on a Scottish heritage float to help celebrate the town's 100th year. (Courtesy Kearny Museum.)

JOHN HARKES. Continuing in the Kearny soccer tradition, John Harkes, a graduate of Kearny High School, played in the World Cup games in 1990 and 1994. In this photograph, taken at Giants Stadium on May 29, 1999, he is No. 6 of the New England Revolution and is playing against No. 16 of the MetroStars, Ramiro Corrales. Harkes's father played professional soccer in Scotland. (Courtesy John Munson/the Star-Ledger.)

HIGHER ED FOR BASEBALL FRED. Perhaps distinguishing himself from many Scottish immigrants, Fred Gillespie chose baseball over soccer. His talent in the sport helped him win a full scholarship to Fairleigh Dickinson University. He served as captain of his college team. Fred later became a teacher, baseball coach, and vice-principal at Kearny High School. (Courtesy Fred Gillespie.)

A ROVING SORT. Duncan MacMillan, a skilled construction worker and veteran of the British Cavalry in World War I, left Scotland and, after employment opportunities in Canada faded, settled in Kearny in the late 1920s. It became obvious that this Scots-Irish town would ultimately become his family's new home in America. (Courtesy Fred Gillespie.)

A DUTIFUL DAUGHTER. In 1929, Duncan MacMillan sent word home to his wife, Catherine, and remaining daughter, six-year-old Jean, that he was on his deathbed and they should come to America as soon as possible. He fully recovered upon their arrival. Jean attended Schuyler School, Lincoln School, and Kearny High School. When her mother became seriously ill, the two sailed for Scotland in 1936. Jean returned to Kearny in 1947. (Courtesy Fred Gillespie.)

DAVID YOUNG. David Young was born in Renfrew, Scotland, in 1860. Before his arrival in America, he served in the Seaforth Highlanders in India and Egypt. He became a naturalized citizen in 1910. The Great Depression caused the foundry where he worked to close. He then became a laborer for the the Kearny town government. While crossing Davis Avenue at the corner of Bergen Avenue in April 1935, he was struck by a car and died a few days later. He is buried at Arlington Cemetery. (Courtesy Bob Kirk.)

MARY GIBSON YOUNG. David Young's wife, Mary, was born in Kilwinning, Ayr County, Scotland, in 1866. She and David married in April 1887 in Paisley, Renfrew County, Scotland. By 1930, she and her family owned their home valued at $7,000 at 213 Bergen Avenue. In 1938, while at her bungalow at Laurence Harbor, she died of a heart attack. (Courtesy George Rogers and Bob Kirk.)

SCOTTISH IMMIGRANTS. David Young arrived in New York on the *Siberian* in 1893. An iron molder by trade, he soon found a job in a steel mill in Harrison and sent for his family. Mary Gibson Young and the couple's three daughters arrived on the *State of Nebraska* later that year. Mary, who had been a thread-mill worker at 14 Thread Street in Paisley, became a thread-mill worker in Kearny as well. (Courtesy George Rogers and Bob Kirk.)

IMMIGRANTS CELEBRATE A WEDDING ANNIVERSARY. Their 40th wedding anniversary in 1928 gave occasion for this photograph of Scottish immigrants David and Mary Gibson Young and their family at 11 Tappan Street. (Courtesy George Rogers.)

AN INDEPENDENT WOMAN. Rachel Young Rogers, daughter of Scottish immigrants, takes a turn on a Harley Davidson in West Hudson Park. (Courtesy George Rogers.)

A HAVEN. The fresh air and open space of West Hudson Park provided a haven from the small, crowded homes at the south end of town that offered no front yards and minimal backyards. The Young children, like many other immigrant offspring, went to the park often to play. (Courtesy George Rogers.)

THE WEST HUDSON PARK CARETAKER. Horticulturist Michael Francis Leahy worked to care for the lands of West Hudson Park. He and his family lived on the property. Here, he stands in the park with Duke Street behind him. (Courtesy the Leahy family.)

LAVINIA PAUL ROGERS. Lavinia Paul was born in England in 1860. She married Alfred Rogers c. 1884 in England and then came to America. They had six children, one of whom died at an early age, and lived at 11 Tappan Street. (Courtesy George Rogers.)

JOHN KIRK. John Kirk was born in Paisley, Scotland, in 1864. At the time of his marriage to Annie Irvine, he was a carpenter. He did a great deal of interior work on the prestigious homes of Newark's Forest Hill section. Later, he became a master mechanic for the McAndrew and Forbes Company, manufacturers of licorice. He was a member and later governor of the St. Andrew's Society of New Jersey. He died after a fall from a ladder in 1926 and is buried in Arlington Cemetery. (Courtesy Bob Kirk.)

ANNIE IRVINE KIRK. Annie Irvine was born in Fermanagh County, Ireland, *c.* 1860 and immigrated to Paisley, Scotland, before journeying to America. She married John Kirk in 1889 in Newark. A homemaker, she is shown here in her backyard at 196 Windsor Street. She died after a tragic fall on a patch of ice in front of Joul's Garage at 385 Kearny Avenue in 1937. (Courtesy Bob Kirk.)

Driving to America? William and Fred Gillespie are prepared to pedal from Scotland to Kearny—all the way from the Rothesay main road—in a car their father made. (Courtesy Fred Gillespie.)

SPURS INSTEAD OF BURRS. It took a while for the Gillespie boys to lose their Scottish burrs. William and Fred, however, exchanged their burrs for cowboy spurs. They attended Garfield School, Washington School, and Kearny High School. (Courtesy Fred Gillespie.)

FROM DUST TO DUST. In a highly emotional moment, Fred and Diane Gillespie place Wilfred's ashes in the waters of Rothesay Bay across from his family home, Westview. The Kearny immigrant had returned home. (Courtesy Fred Gillespie.)

THE GILLESPIE BOYS RETURN TO SCOTLAND. Kearny's Scottish immigrants established a flourishing culture around them with strong ties to their homeland. In 2003, William, Fred, and George Gillespie traveled to Scotland to rediscover their roots. They stand here at Glasgow Airport. (Courtesy Fred Gillespie.)

THE STEWART FAMILY, C. 1940. Thomas Dunlap Stewart and his family are shown in front of their Belgrove Drive residence. Emigrating from Aberdeen, Scotland, the Stewart family initially resided in Massachusetts before settling in Kearny by 1920. Family members are, from left to right, as follows: (front row) George; (middle row) William, Barbara Hewitson Stewart, Thomas Dunlap Stewart, and John; (back row) James, Frank, and Thomas. (Courtesy Craig Stewart.)

43

A FAMOUS SCOT. Jock Nisbet and his son, Colin, pose with Scotsman Sean Connery at the Tavern on the Green. Connery was in Manhattan to accept the New York Film Critics Circle Award. (Courtesy Jock Nisbet.)

REMEMBERING THE SCOTS. Kearny commemorates its Scottish immigrants at Wallace Glen at Riverbank Park. (Courtesy Susan Leahy Jutkiewicz.)

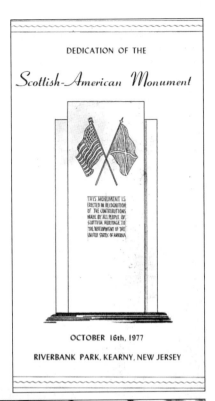

DEDICATION OF THE

Scottish-American Monument

THIS MONUMENT IS ERECTED IN RECOGNITION OF THE CONTRIBUTIONS MADE BY ALL PEOPLE OF SCOTTISH HERITAGE TO THE DEVELOPMENT OF THE UNITED STATES OF AMERICA

OCTOBER 16th, 1977

RIVERBANK PARK, KEARNY, NEW JERSEY

THE CAIRN. In the Scottish tradition, a cairn, or pile of stones, was erected in Wallace Glen. The cairn symbolizes the time when a man embarking on an uncertain voyage placed a stone on such a pile before he left his village. If he returned, he claimed his stone. If he did not, it remained as a memorial. The Kearny cairn represents the Scottish immigrants who left home and the Scots who left Kearny. (Courtesy Susan Leahy Jutkiewicz.)

45

THE SCOTTISH AMERICAN MONUMENT. On October 16, 1977, master of ceremonies James Aitken led the dedication of the Scottish American Monument at Kearny Riverbank Park's Wallace Glen. The monument includes a quote from Woodrow Wilson, "Every line of strength in our history is a line colored by Scottish Blood." (Courtesy Susan Leahy Jutkiewicz.)

THE IRISH HERITAGE MONUMENT. Situated in Kearny Riverbank Park along Passaic Avenue, Irish Heritage Park was dedicated to Rev. Msgr. Joseph A. Carroll on May 19, 1985, and sponsored by the Ancient Order of Hibernians, Division 7. The park features a monument, a plaque of the committee and patrons, a dedication marker, and a memorial to Eileen Ann Kenna, Esq., who served as assistant Hudson County prosecutor from 1984 to 1994.

Two
SWEDEN AND GERMANY

LOUIS LINDBLOM'S BUSINESS. Oral tradition dictates that Swedish immigrant Louis Lindblom, who settled in Arlington in 1879, was responsible for inviting friends and family to join him and thus started the town's Swedish community. (Courtesy Kearny Museum.)

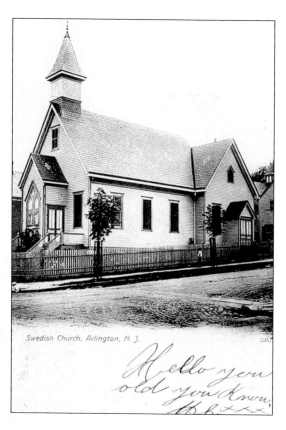

Swedish Church, Arlington, N. J.

Hello you old you know K R xxx

THE FIRST SWEDISH BAPTIST CHURCH OF ARLINGTON. At its height, the town's Swedish population worshiped at one of three churches that conducted services in Swedish. The Baptists separated from the Union's Swedish-language services to form their own church in August 1889. By 1915, the church had 290 members. The church changed names in the 1940s to the Oakwood Avenue Baptist Church due to the decrease of Swedish-speaking people. It is located on the corner of Oakwood and Forrest Streets. (Courtesy Norman Prestup.)

INSIDE THE CHURCH, 1916. Seen is a rare view of the Swedish Lutheran church's interior at Christmastime. (Courtesy First Evangelical Lutheran Church.)

THE ORGANIZATION OF THE LUTHERAN CHURCH. Led by Johan Fredrik Dahllof of Göteborg, Sweden, the Lutherans split from the Union of Swedes of different faiths in Arlington. The organization of the Swedish Evangelical Lutheran Church of Gustavus Vasa finalized on November 9, 1890, with 20 communicants, including the families Dahllof, Palmer, Jacobson, Hanson, Carlson, Sandström, Knutson, Håkansson, Johanson, and Bult. The church secured ground on Elm Street, 50 feet from the corner of Oakwood Avenue, in 1891. Charles A. Pearson presented this photograph "to Herman Peterson for steady attendance to Sunday School for the year 1916." (Courtesy First Evangelical Lutheran Church.)

THE 1915 CONFIRMATION CLASS. The church proudly displays available annual confirmation photographs. This one from 1915 includes, from left to right, the following: (front row) Napthalia Johnson, Ruth Balder Enstice, Pastor Ostlund, Hulda Nordenberg Bermann, and Hedvig Olson Carlen; (back row) Herman Nystrom, Clarence Hoffer, and Walter Olson. (Courtesy First Evangelical Lutheran Church.)

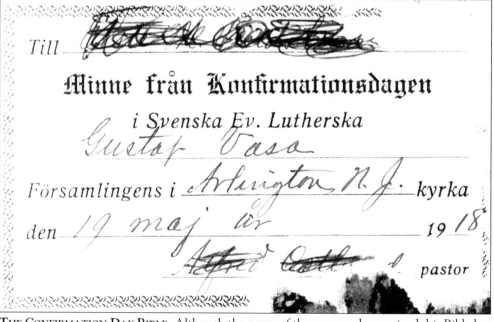

THE CONFIRMATION DAY BIBLE. Although the name of the person who received this Bible has been crossed out, it is clear this Swedish-language Bible was presented on May 19, 1918, by Pastor Alfred Ostlund of the Swedish Lutheran church. (Courtesy Kearny Museum.)

Hemmets Vän

KYRKOTIDNING FÖR FÖRSTA LUTHERSKA FÖRSAMLINGEN I ARLINGTON, N. J.

| ARLINGTON, N. J., | MAJ, 1927 | No. 8 |

THE OFFICIAL BOARD OF THE FIRST EV. LUTHERAN CHURCH IN ARLINGTON, N. J.

Lower row, left to right—Edwin Anderson, Ernest Carlson, G. F. Thompson, Pastor Alfred Ostlund
A. H. Johanson, Emil E. Hollander och Oscar Peterson
Upper row—John Peterson, G. Philipson, Thomas Thompson, Miss Edith Ullman, Walter A. Ullman
Sven Walstrom och Oscar Anderson

PINGST.

Om Pingsten hämta vi följande uppgifter från "Handbok i Biblisk fornkunskap" av C. W. Skarstedt: "På den femtionde dagen eller passah-dagen var veckohögtiden eller, som vi kalla den, pingsten, av judarna tillika kallad förstlingarnas dag och skördefästen. Pingst kommer av grekiska ordet pentekoste, som betyder den femtionde [dagen], men veckohögtid eller [de sju] "veckornas högtid" hette den av de sju veckor, som förflöto från påsk till pingst. Hela denna tid, som utgjorde judarnas skördetid, be-

THE SWEDISH LUTHERAN NEWSLETTER. This May 1927 newsletter, written entirely in Swedish, shows the official board of the First Evangelical Lutheran Church in Arlington. The church had officially modified its name to exclude specific reference to Swedes on April 25, 1927. (Courtesy First Evangelical Lutheran Church.)

THE HÅKANSSON (HAWKINSON) FAMILY. Erik Theodore Håkansson was born in the Swedish village of Krank Lösa in 1874. A machinist, he came to America in 1902 and obtained work with Worthington Pump. He married Judith Regina Johansson, whom he had known in Stockholm, in 1905 and moved to Kearny. They lived at five different addresses in Kearny but spent most of their time at 68 Duke Street and 194 Devon Street. Their sons, Alfred and Arthur, were born at their Duke Street residence in 1906 and 1913, respectively. Arthur is the boy with his finger in his pocket. (Courtesy Arthur Hawkinson.)

MR. JACOBSON. Labeled only as "Mr. Jacobson," this portrait may well have been of Anders Vilhelm Felix Jacobson, one of the first communicants of the Swedish Lutheran church. (Courtesy First Evangelical Lutheran Church.)

MRS. JACOBSON. This portrait may well have been of Emma Louisa Jacobson, née Anderson, one of the first communicants of the Swedish Lutheran church. (Courtesy First Evangelical Lutheran Church.)

THE NEW CHURCH. Swedish architect Martin Hedmark drew plans in 1925 for the new Swedish Evangelical Lutheran Church adjoining the parsonage on Oakwood Avenue, just west of Kearny Avenue. (Courtesy First Evangelical Lutheran Church.)

SWEDISH INSPIRATION IN ARLINGTON. The distinguishing feature of the Hedmark design was a free-standing steeple, referred to commonly as the gateway, inspired by entrances to medieval graveyards adjoining the churches in Sweden. (Courtesy First Evangelical Lutheran Church.)

REVEREND SWENSON. Rev. N.W. Swenson served as pastor of the Swedish Evangelical Lutheran Church from 1901 to 1907. (Courtesy First Evangelical Lutheran Church.)

THE PLAY IS THE THING. In a convenient alcove within the church, the church play group stops their entertainment to pose. (Courtesy First Evangelical Lutheran Church.)

AXEL AND HILMA BJORKEN. Hilma Marie Nilsson, born in 1889 in Malmö, Sweden, immigrated to America in 1905 and lived with an aunt in New York City. Johan "Axel" Bjorken, born in 1888 in Uppsala, Sweden, immigrated in 1909 and got work in a Staten Island laundry. He had read Western magazines while in Sweden and dreamed of becoming a cowboy until he discovered what a cowboy actually did. Instead, he got a job as a billboard painter in Montana. General Outdoor Advertising bought the company he worked for and transferred him to New York City. There, he met Hilma, and they married in 1917. They moved to 13 Trinity Place in Kearny in 1920. (Courtesy Harold Bjorken.)

MAKING IT PERMANENT. Axel Bjorken, kneeling and in overalls, works with another man to cement the new walk to his home. Hilma Bjorken holds their first child, Eric, born in 1920. The Bjorkens attended the Swedish Lutheran church on Oakwood Avenue and, like many of their Swedish friends, were members of the Vasa Lodge on Kearny Avenue. (Courtesy Harold Bjorken.)

TRINITY PLACE. Axel Bjorken stands on the front porch of his new home in Kearny. (Courtesy Harold Bjorken.)

IN THE BACKYARD, C. 1924. Hilma Bjorken and her two older sons, Eric and Allan (born in 1922), enjoy time outside with their dog. (Courtesy Harold Bjorken.)

THE GREAT AMERICAN PASTIME, C. 1929. The Bjorken boys—Eric, Harold, and Allan—are ready for a game of baseball. (Courtesy Harold Bjorken.)

AT LAURENCE HARBOR. In 1934, the Ladies Aid society, which had organized in 1923, traveled to Laurence Harbor, a popular seaside spot for Kearnians, to visit Mrs. Peterson, the mother of Lillie Bjorn and Elsa Peterson. Several men, including Pastor Alfred Ostlund, shown in the top row on the far right, accompanied the ladies. (Courtesy First Evangelical Lutheran Church.)

A SELF PORTRAIT. Photographer Charles A. Pearson artistically created this photographic postcard of himself. (Courtesy First Evangelical Lutheran Church.)

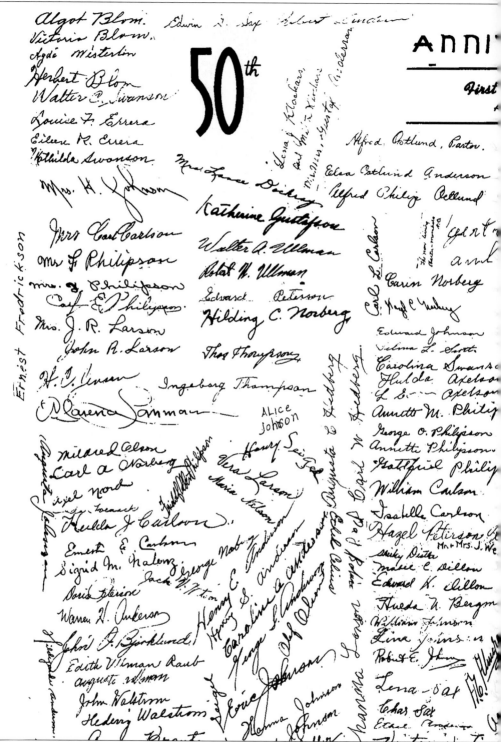

THE 50TH ANNIVERSARY. The Swedish heritage is clear in the signatures of the First Lutheran Church members in the church's 50th anniversary program in 1940. (Courtesy First Evangelical

ARY

rch

Berta Ostlund

Ostlund Anderson

Osclund Bernhard

mrs Ian Johnson

anda L. Peterson

ar Carlson

ie Peterson

Nordenborg

Nordenborg

Backman

Benson

L. Benson

Johnson

Johnson

Anderson

Anderson

Granberg

R. Granberg mrs

t Granberg Jr

Walstrom

d Magnuson

K. Ullman

O. Ullman

Lindby

efen Lindby

a C. D

Iris Faith
Emma Malmay
Ophelia Ford O Nygaard
Mr Harold E Nygaard

Edla Marie Harman
Harold Richard Holman
Mildred Walter Holman
Eric Arnold Malburg Holman

Marie Sylvester
Dorothy Sylvester
Mathilde H

Thelma Johnson Snow

Blythe Davidson

Mrs Clara Swanson

Ernest Linberg
Elsie Larson
Edward J Larson
Mac D Thompson
Walter Falck jr.

Clara S Weden

Emil E Hollander
Elvin Hollander
Raymond E. Hollander
Lillian Hollander
Frances Hollander
Minnie Hollander
Clara C. Hoffer
Peter W. Hoffer
J. R. Franzin
Elizabeth P. Ericsson
Eric Ericsson
Hilda Peterson
Mrs Emily

Verner Anderson Clifford H. Anderson

Clay Lindbergh
Mae Lindbergh
Dagmar Lindbergh
Ollie Sax
Carl D. Carlson
Florence Celus
Helen Celus
Esther H. Eberhard
Carl Sax

Carlyan Byers
Robert Larson

Clara Larson
Ruth Larson
Mrs. George Hankin
Elsie Larson

Mr & Mrs O Schumacher
Edward B Schumacher
Hannah B
Chester L Anderson
Oscar Peterson
Mrs Oscar Peterson
Mr & Mrs. H. M. Peterson
Astrid Olson
Mr & Mrs. C. Olson
Mrs. M. Sylvester
Yvonne B. Nelson
Walter A Nelson
Mrs Hattie Johnson
Linda Johnson
Ed Wernes
Alice Wernes
Roy W. Nelson
Idof Lindberg
Erik Billing
Selma Billing

Lutheran Church.)

61

BUSY, BUSY. These boys are hard at work at Christmastime in 1954. (Courtesy First Evangelical Lutheran Church.)

EXERCISE, ANYONE? Schoolchildren take a stretch break from their studies at Christmastime in 1954. (Courtesy First Evangelical Lutheran Church.)

KARL NORDBERG, C. 1900. Born in 1878 in Sweden, Karl Albin Karlson Nordberg arrived in America in 1903. He stayed in Kearny with his mother on Beech Street near Laurel Avenue. He worked as a pipe fitter for DuPont on Schuyler Avenue until his retirement in 1947. (Courtesy Rita Norberg.)

KARIN (CARIN) HED, C. 1900. Karin Hed, from Hudiksvall on the coast north of Stockholm, stayed with the Erickson family when she arrived in Kearny in 1907. She and Karl Nordberg (which at some point became Norberg) married in 1908 in the Swedish Lutheran church. She and her sister were the only family members to come to America. (Courtesy Rita Norberg.)

Three Generations of Swedish Heritage. Three generations of Norbergs—Karl (later Carl), his mother, and his daughter Hazel—enjoy the outdoors. (Courtesy Rita Norberg.)

The Norberg Children, c. 1923–1924. George (left), Hilding (center), and Hazel Norberg were all born at home. George married Scottish immigrant Rita Morton. Hilding married Shirley Jacobson, the daughter of Kearny Swedish immigrants. Hazel worked for West Hudson Hospital for 40 years. (Courtesy Rita Norberg.)

JACOB STUMPF. In 1912, Jacob Stumpf, born in Hesse-Cassel, Germany, in 1839, donated his residence and several surrounding lots to found a hospital on the corner of Bergen Avenue and Elm Street in memory of his wife, the late Mary Hahn. It was called Jacob Stumpf Memorial Hospital and it opened in October 1913 with 36 beds and a medical staff of 12 physicians and surgeons. Stumpf was in business with his father-in-law at the Hahn & Stumpf leather tanning factory in Harrison. He died in 1913. (Courtesy Gordon Kimball.)

HENRY KARL MARTIN SPRENGEL. Born in 1863 in the German port city of Hamburg, Henry Karl Martin Sprengel came to America in the 1890s. He found work as a stock clerk. He and his wife, Berta Brenner (also from Germany), met aboard ship, married *c.* 1895, and moved to Kearny's Devon Street in 1907. In New Jersey, he worked as a machinist at Worthington Pump. (Courtesy Joan Sprengel Kimball.)

THE SPRENGEL FAMILY. Multiple generations of the Sprengel family take respite on the porch steps for this photograph. (Courtesy Joan Sprengel Kimball.)

Three

LITHUANIA

OUR LADY'S SODALITY CHOIR, 1948. Traditional costumes add to the beauty of this female choir. The organization from which the choir was formed was established in 1946 and 10 years later boasted 88 members. (Courtesy Our Lady of Sorrows Church.)

THE HOLY NAME SOCIETY. When Our Lady of Sorrows parish was formed in 1916, the first to organize were the men of the Lithuanian Holy Name Society. Its first spiritual advisor was Reverend Jakstys, and the first president was Mamertas Kauklys. The Holy Name Society, shown here in October 1938, was responsible for the construction of the new Our Lady of Sorrows Church at the corner of Davis and Bergen Avenues. (Courtesy Our Lady of Sorrows Church.)

FR. LEO VOICIEKAUSKAS. Born in Iglauka, Lithuania, in 1892, Leo Voiciekauskas served as Our Lady of Sorrows Church's fourth pastor, from 1931 to 1963. With his guidance, the parish flourished, forming many organizations and building a new church to accommodate the growing community. He poses here (on the left in the back row) with children who, as described in the church's 50th anniversary book, "came under his magnetic spell." (Courtesy Our Lady of Sorrows Church.)

A FLAG FOR INDEPENDENCE. Lithuanians have called Kearny home since at least 1895. To celebrate the day on which Lithuania gained its independence—February 16, 1918—the raising of the Lithuanian flag takes place at Kearny's town hall. Shown here is community leader Matt Sluzis (on the right in the fur cap) as master of ceremonies for the flag raising on Lithuania Day in 1978. (Courtesy Our Lady of Sorrows Church.)

FATHER POCUS. Instructing children in Lithuanian language and culture as well as in religion has long been important to Kearny's Lithuanian community. Fr. Dominick Pocus poses here with children from Our Lady of Sorrows Church in 1948. (Courtesy Our Lady of Sorrows Church.)

THE NEW CHURCH BREAKS GROUND. The parish decided to move to a more centralized location in Kearny, the corner of Bergen and Davis Avenues, from Harrison. The new church building fund launched on October 26, 1952. Groundbreaking ceremonies were held at the new site, shown above on August 30, 1953, with Father Voiciekauskas presiding. The cornerstone ceremony took place on March 20, 1954. (Courtesy Our Lady of Sorrows Church.)

OUR LADY OF SORROWS LITHUANIAN ROMAN CATHOLIC CHURCH. The Our Lady of Sorrows parish was established to satisfy emotional and social demands as well as religious needs. The parish formally established in 1915 to serve 700 Lithuanians in Harrison and 400 in Kearny. On the occasion of the parish's 50th anniversary, Reverend Pocus wrote, "Second- and third-generation families may never fully appreciate the fervent longings of their forebears for the sights and sounds of their homeland. But certainly our older parishioners can recall the poverty of our people, their loneliness in a strange land, their youth and energy, and feeling of unity which they felt with their fellow Lithuanians." (Courtesy Our Lady of Sorrows Church.)

PETER W. VELEVAS. Peter W. Velevas served as councilman for Kearny's second ward. (Courtesy Elena Nakrosis.)

JOHN J. SALVEST. A Kearny attorney, John J. Salvest also served as a municipal judge. (Courtesy Elena Nakrosis.)

The Schuyler Savings Bank. The Schuyler Building and Loan Association opened in 1924 to help the Lithuanian immigrant community become financially independent. Notably, the bank provided a mortgage to the new Lithuanian Catholic Community Center (LCCC) at 6 Davis Avenue in 1939. (Courtesy Elena Nakrosis.)

Schuyler Savings Bank Officials. Seen here are, from left to right, the following: (front row) P. Velevas, A. Salvest, J. Paknis, C. Paulis, and J. Belza; (back row) W. Shukis, C. Nakrosis, G. Katilus, S.A. Mickewich, G. Bezgela, V. Mikionis, M. Churinskas, and W. Plikaitis. (Courtesy Elena Nakrosis.)

BEATRICE KAZALIS, 1955.
Lithuanian Beatrice Kazalis and her family lived at 251 Schuyler Avenue. The vine leaves over her right shoulder are hops leaves, used in the manufacture of beer during Prohibition. The home served as a speakeasy. There was a candy store in the front and immigrant laborers walked through the candy store into Beatrice's kitchen, where she sold them homemade beer and whiskey. (Courtesy James Kazalis.)

THE ST. ANN'S SOCIETY. This society was one of the many organizations affiliated with Kearny's Lithuanian community. Fr. Leo Voiciekauskas organized it in 1932. Its objective was to work for the church and Lithuanian nation. (Courtesy Our Lady of Sorrows Church.)

THE LITH CLUB. No longer in existence, Schuyler Avenue's Lith Club served as the home of the Lithuanian-American political club. (Courtesy Elena Nakrosis.)

THE LITHUANIAN CATHOLIC COMMUNITY CENTER (LCCC). Members of the Holy Name Society established the LCCC in 1939 and purchased the building at 6 Davis Avenue. Offering the largest hall in the Kearny area, it has been a home for Lithuanian events and organizational meetings. It is also used by other groups and serves as a popular site for showers and weddings. (Courtesy Elena Nakrosis.)

THE KNIGHTS OF LITHUANIA, 1947. Organized in 1917, the Kearny-Harrison chapter did its part in the 1940s to aid the national organization in its mission to help Lithuania achieve independence. Father Pocus sits in the middle of the front row. The chapter also sponsored a baseball team and a basketball team. Today, the chapter sends sorely needed medical supplies to Lithuania. (Courtesy Elena Nakrosis.)

THE LITHUANIAN DANCE TROUPE, C. 1970. Elena Nakrosis organized this group of Kearny youngsters, including her own children, to perform in the town's cultural events and throughout New Jersey. (Courtesy Elena Nakrosis.)

Four

GREECE, ITALY, AND PORTUGAL

WAITING FOR EMIGRATION. A group gathers in the Greek port of Pireas to see the Mihalis family off to America in April 1963. (Courtesy Christina Mihalis Kozinski.)

A GREEK CLASSIC. At 16 years old, Alexandros Golematis left his native town, Thisbe (meaning "the village of doves"), in Greece in June 1952 to travel by sea to Hoboken, New Jersey. He received his visa to enter the United States under the Orphan Law. (Courtesy Christina Mihalis Kozinski.)

BROTHER AND SISTER. Alex's sister, Panagioula, who had also come to America in 1952 under the Orphan Law, returned to Greece in 1958 and married George Vlachos. The newlyweds settled in Kearny. (Courtesy Christina Mihalis Kozinski.)

AN INVITATION TO JOIN. Alex Golematis worked in the Sunflower Restaurant in Jersey City, where his bosses—three brothers also from Greece—liked him. Chris, John, and Nick Dominos and Nick Glynos asked Golematis to become a partner in a new diner at the corner of River Road and the Belleville Turnpike. From left to right are Alex Golematis, Nick Dominos, and Chris Dominos. (Courtesy Christina Mihalis Kozinski.)

THE ARLINGTON DINER OPENS. This new diner opened in June 1958 and was appropriately called the Arlington Diner. (Courtesy Christina Mihalis Kozinski.)

INSIDE THE DINER. Proud owners, Greek immigrants Nick Dominos (left), Alex Golematis (center), and John Dominos pose for the camera. (Courtesy Christina Mihalis Kozinski.)

DANCING IN THE DINER. There was more to the Arlington Diner than just food. Clear the tables and move aside for a traditional Greek dance. (Courtesy Christina Mihalis Kozinski.)

INSIDE THE KITCHEN. Alex Golematis takes a moment of rest from his hectic restaurant life in the diner's kitchen. (Courtesy Christina Mihalis Kozinski.)

GRANDMA'S GIRLS, C. 1965. Four girls surround their grandmother. From left to right are Christina Mihalis, Alexandra Golematis (holding Alexandra Vlachos), Konstantina Vlachos, and Alexandra Golematis. Alex Golematis brought his mother, Alexandra, to America when he returned from Greece with his bride, Voula Nokas, in 1961. (Courtesy Christina Mihalis Kozinski.)

THE MIHALISES. Alex's sister, Eleni, and Eleni's husband, Loukas Mihalis, traveled on the *Olympia* to America in 1963, joining their friends and family in Kearny. (Courtesy Christina Mihalis Kozinski.)

FOUR ROSES, 1954. Infant Roseanne Carchidi is surrounded by her mother, Rose M.A. Carchidi, who settled on Devon Street; her grandmother, Rose M. Carchidi; and her great-grandmother, Rose Lombardi. (Courtesy Roseanne Carchidi Stewart.)

THE CARCHIDI WEDDING, 1927. F. Saverio (1895–1969) from Calabria, Italy, met and married Rose M. Carchidi (1908–1982) of Brockton, Massachusetts. The newlyweds made their home on Devon Street south of Stewart Avenue and raised four children: Clara, Rose, Vincent, and Joseph. The ring bearer is Joseph Lombardi and the flower girl is Rose Yanni. Also shown are Joseph Carchidi and Anna Lombardi. (Courtesy Roseanne Carchidi Stewart.)

MAYOR HEALY CUTS THE RIBBON. Proud owners Joseph Coccia Jr. and his wife, Elda, hold up their ends of the ribbon in the grand opening ceremony of the Coccia Agency in 1961. (Courtesy Chris Coccia.)

THE COCCIA AGENCY. Owner Joseph Coccia Jr. came to Kearny in the late 1950s from Kossuth Street in Newark, where his Italian immigrant father had settled. The Coccia Agency has served the real-estate and insurance needs of the Kearny area for more than 40 years. (Courtesy Chris Coccia.)

ROCCO DeCARLUCCI. Born in 1881, Rocco DeCarlucci came to America first and then sent for his wife, his first cousin, Carmela. A carpenter, he lived at 40 Johnston Avenue and died in 1963. (Courtesy the Leahy family.)

CARMELA DeCARLUCCI. Born in Salerno, Italy, in 1889, Carmela DeCarlucci followed her husband to America, entering through Philadelphia c. 1921. (Courtesy the Leahy family.)

NICOLA RASPA. Nicola Raspa left his home in Gasperina in the Italian province of Calabria to seek work in America. He came to the Kearny area because his wife's brother lived in Harrison. Here, he stands in front of his shoe-repair shop. Over a 10-year period, he continually sent money back to his family. Finally, in 1939, as war broke out in Europe, he brought his family here. (Courtesy Marianne Jacullo Brosnan.)

MARIA RASPA. Nicola's daughter Maria arrived in Kearny at the age of 17 in 1939. Having worked in a bridal shop in Italy, she found work in a coat factory in East Newark. There she met pattern cutter Emil Jacullo, whom she married in 1948. (Courtesy Marianne Jacullo Brosnan.)

"BUSTER" VISCUSO. Shown here with his wife, Millie, and children, Frank and Anna, Sebastiano "Buster" Viscuso owned Buster's Market at 57 Kearny Avenue. The family lived above the store. He arrived in America at the age of 18 in 1923 to join his uncle Mauro in Harrison. (Courtesy Maurice Viscuso.)

THE CRISTALDI FAMILY. Charlie Cristaldi owned Charlie's Market at 152 Kearny Avenue. He and his wife, the former Palma Viscuso, both Sicilian immigrants, lived with their children— John, Maurice, Nancy, and Charlie—at 19 Pavonia Avenue. (Courtesy Maurice Viscuso.)

ON THE TOWN IN THE LATE 1930S. Brothers Sebastian Viscuso (left) and Salvatore Viscuso (right) enjoy a dinner out in New York with their wives, the former Mary Sloan and Fae Lacarra. The brothers owned the Evergreen Market at 572 Kearny Avenue. Sebastian and Mary resided on Forest Street, and Sal and Fae lived on South Midland Avenue. Their father, Mauro, came from Aci Castello, Sicily, *c.* 1900 and owned a small produce store in Harrison. (Courtesy Maurice Viscuso.)

TONY MEOLA. Continuing the tradition of his father, who had played professional soccer in Italy, Belleville-born Meola played soccer for Kearny High School (with teammate John Harkes) and went on to play in the 1990 and 1994 World Cup games as goalkeeper. He is recognized as one of the top goalkeepers in major-league soccer and now plays for the Kansas City Wizards. Here, he winces in pain after making a first-half save against the Los Angeles Galaxy at Giants Stadium in 1998. (Courtesy Andrew Mills/the Star-Ledger.)

BILLY GONSALVES, "THE BABE RUTH OF AMERICAN SOCCER." Born in Rhode Island in 1907 to Portuguese immigrant parents from the island of Madeira, Adelino Gonsalves, nicknamed "Billy" by his English and Scottish soccer mates, represented the United States in the World Cup in 1930 and 1934. He lived at 48 Columbia Avenue and played with Kearny's Scots-American team in 1941–1942. He entered the National Soccer Hall of Fame in its first year, 1950. He died in Kearny in 1977. (Courtesy Kearny Museum.)

PORTUGAL DAY. In 1978, a group of Kearny residents decided to celebrate a day in June for the Portuguese with a church ceremony, parade, and flag raising in front of town hall. The reaction to the first Portugal Day was so overwhelming that residents decided to form a cultural organization. (Courtesy Portuguese Cultural Association.)

THE PORTUGUESE CULTURAL ASSOCIATION. Associação Cultural Portuguesa, the Portuguese Cultural Association, formed in 1979 with a charter to maintain the culture, tradition, and customs of their original Portuguese ancestors while helping future generations understand and learn about their heritage. The association established itself in this building on Schuyler Avenue. (Courtesy Portuguese Cultural Association.)

THE DIRECTORS, 1980–1984. Seen are the first directors of the Portuguese Cultural Association. They are, from left to right, as follows: (front row) J. Ataide, J. Costa, J. Casimiro, V. Santos, F. Bacalhau, and A. Santiago; (middle row) D. Morais, A. Neno, L. Pereira, F. Raposo, R. Raposo, A. Castro, I. Nogueira, and M. Martins; (back row) F. Cardoza, J. Pinho, E. Duarte, A. Cardoso, L. Pereira, M. Leques, J. Oliveira, J. Gonçalves, F. Lourenço, and J. Laranjeiro. Not pictured are B. Santos, V. Rua, F. Rua, J. Matos, and M. Santiago. (Courtesy Portuguese Cultural Association.)

PORTUGAL DAY, 1985. Mayor Hill officiates Portugal Day on June 2, 1985. (Courtesy Portuguese Cultural Association.)

A PORTUGAL DAY PAUSE. The celebration pauses for a photograph behind town hall. (Courtesy Portuguese Cultural Association.)

A LITTLE MUSIC. Accordion players serenade Portugal Day participants in town hall's plaza. (Courtesy Portuguese Cultural Association.)

FLOATING ALONG KEARNY AVENUE. Portugal Day celebrants ride along atop this gaily decorated float during the parade. (Courtesy Portuguese Cultural Association.)

A GREAT DAY FOR A PARADE. Holding the Kearny Portuguese American Club banner is no problem for these three. Note the Portuguese flag emblems worn by the men on the left. (Courtesy Portuguese Cultural Association.)

PROUD TO BE PORTUGUESE. These three girls announce the coming of the Portuguese Cultural Association of Kearny in a Newark St. Patrick's Day parade. (Courtesy Portuguese Cultural Association.)

THE DREAMS OF PORTUGAL. In 1980, Agostinho Cardoso, originally from Portugal's northern region of Minho, approached the founders of the Portuguese Cultural Association with the idea of starting up a folklore dance group similar to those found in Portugal. With their approval, he began to recruit volunteers, shown here. The group became known as the Dreams of Portugal. (Courtesy Portuguese Cultural Association.)

KICK UP YOUR HEELS. Mayor Vartan participates in the annual dinner dance of the Portuguese Cultural Association. (Courtesy Portuguese Cultural Association.)

A DAY IN NEW YORK. In April 2002, Fox's *Good Day New York* program included a segment on the Portuguese community that featured representatives of Kearny's Portuguese Cultural Association. (Courtesy Portuguese Cultural Association.)

CHILDREN ARE THE FUTURE. Karlee Rodrigues and Kyle Barbosa hold hands at an association celebration. (Courtesy Portuguese Cultural Association.)

LIBERTY FOR ALL. Dreams of Portugal performs at the 50th anniversary of the anti-defamation league at Liberty State Park. (Courtesy Portuguese Cultural Association.)

AN ANNIVERSARY YEAR. Mayor Alberto Santos (right) stands at the Portuguese Club in Newark with Paulo Pocinho, the city's highest-ranking Portuguese official. (Courtesy Portuguese Cultural Association.)

THE PORTUGAL DAY PLATFORM. Mayor Santos (fourth from the left) observes the celebration from an elevated vantage point. (Courtesy Portuguese Cultural Association.)

THE PORTUGUESE SCHOOL, 1999. Twice a week after school, Portuguese children trek to Lincoln School for Ecola Portuguesa—education in Portuguese language and culture. (Courtesy Portuguese Cultural Association.)

SCHOOL IS OUT! The Portuguese school's 2003 graduating class celebrates with a cake at a favorite restaurant. (Courtesy Portuguese Cultural Association.)

A Soccer Team. Attempts were made to create and maintain an association soccer team, shown here in 1983. (Courtesy Portuguese Cultural Association.)

Track and Field. Although soccer did not pan out, track and field did. The team is shown here in 2000. (Courtesy Portuguese Cultural Association.)

MISS PORTUGUESE CULTURAL ASSOCIATION. Each year, a teenaged girl is chosen to represent the club. (Courtesy Portuguese Cultural Association.)

THE FUTURE MAYOR. Domingos Santos and Doralice Craco were born in the Portuguese village of Murtosa. Shortly after marrying in 1954, the emigrated from Portugal to Caracas, Venezuela. Alberto Santos, now Kearny's mayor, was born in Venezuela in 1965. In 1970, the family—including Alberto's sister, Doralice, who had been living with grandparents in Portugal—moved to the United States. In 1979, they moved to Kearny, as it was a pleasant and attractive community close to work in Newark. Pictured here are, from left to right, mother Doralice, Domingos, Doralice, and Alberto in 1970 with their Delta 88 car. (Courtesy Alberto Santos.)

Five
LATIN AMERICA

URUGUAY INDEPENDENCE. Gabriela Raffo-Castillo left Montevideo, Uruguay, in 1980 with her parents and brother to join her uncle in Kearny. They are part of the town's growing Uruguayan community that now numbers about 200. Here, she stands with the Uruguay flag at Sacred Heart School's gymnasium on Wilson Street as the community prepares to celebrate the August 25 Uruguay independence.

TAB RAMOS. Born in Montevideo, Uruguay, Tab Ramos followed in his father's professional soccer footsteps. He came to America at age 11 in 1978 and became a U.S. citizen in 1982. Kearny became his home. He participated in three World Cup games—1990, 1994, and 1998—and plays for the MetroStars. A popular face in U.S. soccer through advertising endorsements for Nike, Snickers, and McDonald's, Ramos also serves as a literacy champion for New Jersey. (Courtesy William Perlman/the Star-Ledger.)

SARA CORDOBA AND FAMILY. Sara Cordoba's family came to America in 1959 from Ecuador and settled in New York City. After many years there and in Astoria, Queens, the family moved to Kearny in the summer of 1982 for more affordable housing and to be with a great-aunt's family. From left to right are Teresa, Rodrigo (holding Otto), Sara, and William. (Courtesy Alexa Arce.)

A CHRISTMAS PORTRAIT. William Cordoba holds baby Sandra next to his siblings Teresa and Otto in this Christmas portrait. Note the family photograph hanging on the wall behind them. (Courtesy Alexa Arce.)

AN ESCAPE FROM COMMUNISM. In 1967, Mayra Santos; her parents, Feliberto and Olaya Guzman; and her sister, Idania, left their home in the mountainous eastern province of Oriente in Castro's Cuba to come to America and freedom. (Courtesy Mayra Santos.)

MANGOS CAFÉ AND RESTAURANT. After working in the accounting department at Mutual Benefit in Newark for 27 years, Mayra Santos decided to open a Cuban restaurant on Kearny Avenue, giving area residents a unique culinary choice. Despite no prior knowledge of the restaurant business, her five-year-old establishment is flourishing as the culmination of an American dream. Santos lived in Kearny from 1981 to 1999.

Six
JAPAN

A DOLL FESTIVAL. Tomiko and Shinako Masui of Devon Street proudly display the family's private doll collection. (Courtesy Tada Yamaguchi.)

VISUAL HISTORY. Hidetaro Yamaguchi was a self-taught artist. In a small booklet, he drew portraits of life in Japan to share with his children. Here, he shows the village of Mizonokuchi,

where his wife and his child Shidzu were born. (Courtesy Tada Yamaguchi.)

THE CHICKENS ON OAKWOOD AVENUE. Hidetaro Yamaguchi, born in Japan in 1873, first came to the United States and made his way to Chicago with his wife and small children. He eventually settled in Kearny, buying a house on Oakwood Avenue. Here, he stands in 1925 with the chickens he raised for eggs. (Courtesy Tada Yamaguchi.)

THE HOUSE GETS A NEW ROOF. The Yamaguchi home at 72 Oakwood still belongs to the family today. Installing a new roof warranted some picture taking. (Courtesy Tada Yamaguchi.)

MOTHER AND CHILD. Shinako Okumura Yamaguchi, born in 1883, holds her first Arlington-born child, Tada, in 1917. Tada later grew up to be the January 1935 Kearny High School class valedictorian. (Courtesy Tada Yamaguchi.)

TWO IMMIGRANTS. Shinako Yamaguchi and neighbor, Canadian-born Lydia Hanwell, lock arms on Oakwood Avenue in the 1920s. (Courtesy Tada Yamaguchi.)

A Home Wedding, 1927. Takeji Kusanobu, the first Japanese immigrant to come to Kearny, offered his Pleasant Place home to host the wedding of fellow immigrant Shikichi "Chick" Masui and his bride, Hatsue. Oral tradition has it that Chick often visited the Yamaguchi house before his marriage for a home-cooked meal. (Courtesy Tomiko Masui.)

THE KUSANOBU HOME. Importer Takeji Kusanobu came to America in 1894 and eventually settled in this home, located at 51 Pleasant Place. (Courtesy Tomiko Masui.)

THE MATSUO FAMILY HOME. The Matsuo family, related to the Masui family through marriage, lived in this house at the corner of Belgrove Drive and Oakwood Avenue. (Courtesy Tomiko Masui.)

THIRD GRADE. Seiko Yamaguchi sits on the far left in the front row of this class picture taken in front of the first Lincoln School on Kearny Avenue. (Courtesy Seiko Yamaguchi.)

CULTURES COMBINE. A Yamaguchi granddaughter, Masako, born in 1934, stands facing the Yamaguchi home with the First Lutheran church, a Swedish church, behind her. (Courtesy Tada Yamaguchi.)

THE YAMAGUCHI FAMILY, 1930. Seen here are, from left to right, the following: (front row) Mitsuo Yamaguchi, Tada Yamaguchi, and Tsugio Yamaguchi; (middle row) Hiroshi Matsuo (holding Taka Yamaguchi), Tsugye Matsuo, Hatsue Masui, Shiga Yamaguchi, and Bobe Yamaguchi; (back row) Shikichi Masui, Kadzuo Yamaguchi, Shidzuko Yamaguchi, Seiko Yamaguchi, Hidetaro Yamaguchi, and Shina Yamaguchi. (Courtesy Tada Yamaguchi.)

EASTER BONNETS. The Yamaguchi girls gather around the back of their home to show-off their Easter bonnets. (Courtesy Tada Yamaguchi.)

EASTER SUNDAY, C. 1935. Family togetherness is the theme of this portrait of the Yamaguchi family on Easter. (Courtesy Tomiko Masui.)

CHERRY BLOSSOM TIME, 1938. The *Newark Sunday Call* featured sisters Tomiko and Shinako Masui in Newark's Branch Brook Park. (Courtesy Tomiko Masui.)

A GOLF OUTING. "Chick" Masui, who worked with Takeji Kusanobu, joined him for this golf outing. (Courtesy Tomiko Masui.)

HIDEKO YAMAGUCHI, C. 1960. Three-year-old "Heidi," the daughter of Tsugio Yamaguchi, poses in traditional dress. (Courtesy Tada Yamaguchi.)

A MEMORIAL TO A CLASSMATE. Heidi Yamaguchi, a 1975 graduate of Kearny High School, found her true passion with canine search and rescue teams. She died of sudden terminal illness in April 2003. Said the Humane Society of the United States in a letter to Heidi's mother, Kimi, "Heidi had her own means of communicating, her own language with dogs. She had a very special ability to train these exceptional performers using the best and most humane methods." She is shown here with Fuyu, one of her many dogs. (Courtesy Tada Yamaguchi.)

WORLD WAR II. U.S. GIs Kadzuo and Tsugio Yamaguchi stand at the American Red Cross in January 1945. During the war, their father, who was not a naturalized U.S. citizen, had been taken to Ellis Island and was later released into the custody of a Mr. McBride. (Courtesy Tada Yamaguchi.)

Seven

THE JEWISH
COMMUNITY

HEBREW SCHOOL STUDENTS. Congregation B'nai Israel of Kearny and North Arlington's spiritual leader, Rabbi Sidney M. Bogner sits with a group of Hebrew school students. (Courtesy Jewish Historical Society of MetroWest.)

THE GROUNDBREAKING CEREMONIES. By the 1950s, Kearny's Jewish congregation outgrew its synagogue on Chestnut Street. Henry Jacobs broke ground as part of the ceremonies for the new Kearny Avenue synagogue that took place on February 7, 1954, escorted by Alex Scheinzeit, the congregation president, and Alex Tauber, the building committee chairman. (Courtesy Jewish Historical Society of MetroWest.)

A NEW HOME. Cornerstone laying ceremonies took place on September 19, 1954. Max Edlin was the chairman of the committee and Rabbi Leon Yagod was the advisor. Other members of the committee were Saul J. Abraham, Samuel Greenstein, Meyer Kellman, Joseph Kook, Al Scheinzeit, Faye Schulman, Al Tauber, and Nathan Winter. (Courtesy Jewish Historical Society of MetroWest.)

KEARNY'S JEWISH COMMUNITY ORGANIZED IN 1913. To celebrate the congregation's 50 years, a dinner dance was held on May 4, 1963. In August 1913, 19 men signed the application for the incorporation of Congregation B'nai Israel of Arlington. They were Samuel Batta, William Brummer, Harry Danziger, Abraham Davimos, Nathan Davimos, Joseph Fine, Philip Glantz, Morris Goldman, Israel Goldstein, Louis Grossman, Max Jaffe, Harry Kaminowitz, Rachmael Kaplan, Samuel Klein, Samuel Kavaleer, Barnet Meisterman, Samuel Salls, Hascher Schnitzer, and Hyman Simchowitz. Israel Goldstein served as the first leader and acting president. (Courtesy Jewish Historical Society of MetroWest.)

You are cordially invited
to attend the
Fiftieth Anniversary Dinner Dance
of
Congregation B'nai Israel
to be held
on Saturday, May fourth
Nineteen hundred and sixty-three
at nine o'clock in the evening

Congregation B'nai Israel
780 Kearny Avenue
Kearny, New Jersey

Reception at eight-thirty o'clock
Cocktails and Hors D'oeuvres

Complete Evening $15.00 per person

1913 - 1963

Fiftieth Anniversary
Dinner Dance
Program

Congregation B'nai Israel
of
Kearny and North Arlington

May 4th, 1963

THE JEWISH COMMUNITY CELEBRATES 50 YEARS. Wrote Jack Golding, the 50th Anniversary Celebration Committee chairman, "There were times of dreams and plans, periods of great effort to make these plans realities and there were times of frustration and discouragement. But always there was the hard core of dedicated men and women of our community that persevered and brought us to this day." (Courtesy Jewish Historical Society of MetroWest.)

HONORED FOR HIS SERVICE. On November 25, 1962, Congregation B'nai Israel of Kearny and North Arlington honored Russian immigrant Jacob Heiligman, who arrived in America in 1904 and owned a dry-goods business on Kearny Avenue. He served for more than 25 years as sexton. Here, he is shown with important congregation members. From left to right are Morris Cohen, Al Scheinzeit, Nat Rogoff, Sol Rogoff, Joel Harrison, Rabbi Sidney Bogner, Jacob Heiligman, Edith Saletan, Milton Bruck, Jack Golding, Joseph Kook, and Max Edlin. (Courtesy Jewish Historical Society of MetroWest.)

REVERED IN PRAISES. Rabbi Sidney M. Bogner served as Kearny's spiritual leader from 1956 to 1974. Born in 1909 to an Austrian rabbinical family, Bogner was active in many Jewish and community associations, including the New Jersey Board of Rabbis. He died in 1986. (Courtesy Jewish Historical Society of MetroWest.)

COMMUNITY TIES. I. Michael Sumner (right) of Hamilton Avenue stands with Dr. Louis Finkelstein, chancellor of the Jewish Theological Seminary of America. Sumner served as president of Congregation B'nai Israel from 1963 to 1965. (Courtesy Jewish Historical Society of MetroWest.)

KRASNER'S SHOP-RITE. Max Krasner arrived in America in 1899 from Borisov, Minsk province, Russia. He moved in 1920 from Newark to Ridge Road in North Arlington, where he and his wife, Eva Zuckerkandel, an immigrant from Austria-Hungary, opened a general store (now the Italian Villa). During the Great Depression, the Krasners developed a reputation for helping patrons weather economic hard times through the extension of store credit. Max and his sons, Milton, Harry, and Herman, opened Krasner's Shop-Rite at 169 Ridge Road in 1953. Max moved to Elizabeth Avenue in Kearny in 1949. Milton and his family moved to Clinton Avenue in 1958.

THE CHILDREN OF IMMIGRANT PARENTS MARRY. Max and Eva Krasner stand on March 25, 1951, with daughter Doris and her new husband, fellow Kearnian Marvin Bartner, whose immigrant parents owned a shop at the south end of town. (Courtesy Doris Bartner.)

THE LEVYS. Shoe business veterans Herbert and Ilse Rothschild Levy left Germany in 1941 and came to America through Portugal on one of the last remaining visas. Herbert had been forced to build roads in a concentration camp. He and Ilse settled in Manhattan. Herbert was offered a choice of three Buster Brown locations. He chose Kearny because of its proximity to New York and family. They came to Kearny in 1954 and opened Wel-Fit Shoes, now owned and operated by their son, Larry. (Courtesy Larry Levy.)

THE ZALKINS. William Zalkin came to America from Russia in 1911. He opened a dry-goods store at 126 Schuyler Avenue. He is shown here with his wife, Sally, and twin daughters, Dorothy and Florence. In 1938, a local newspaper called Zalkin "the Bamberger of Kearny," with "a brilliant reputation for service and satisfaction, for supplying quality merchandise at pleasing prices." (Courtesy Norman Prestup.)

ZALKIN'S LUMBER. In March 1938, Bill Zalkin broke ground for a new building to be constructed at Schuyler Avenue and Hoyt Street. This was to be an annex to house a burgeoning supply of building materials. Bill Zalkin and his daughter Dorothy stand in the doorway in this publicity shot. (Courtesy Norman Prestup.)